ROOTS OF A GIRL

Meghan Hughes

Meghan Hughes
Philadelphia, PA

Cover Design @2025 Lara Fowler @TheQuoteHouse
Illustrations @2025 Blumen Soul
Book Layout ©2017 BookDesignTemplates.com

Ordering Information:
Quantity sales. Special discounts are available on quantity purchases by corporations, associations, and others. For details, contact the author at www.MeghanHughesWriting.com

Roots of a Girl/ Meghan Hughes. -- 1st ed.
ISBN 979-8-9920470-0-4

Praise for Roots of a Girl

"**This collection of poetry reads as if Hughes is sitting next to you at her own dining room table.** In front of you are spread a scattering of memories, feelings, griefs large and small. She invites you to pick one up. You do, carefully, touching only the edges, and read. You feel. You ache. She writes of particular moments in time that ring universal, that touch on your own life and echo back to each other. While Meghan's poetry is uniquely her own, everyone can see pieces of themselves in her collection. **A must read if you're craving introspection and connection, which the world needs more of.**"

- Sophie Laine

"Through the exploration of a life of traumas and human moments, *Roots of a Girl* ebbs and flows through the process of healing, without shying away from all its joyous victories and bitter defeats...the change and growth is nearly tangible with how gripped you'll be by it. **No matter who you are, or where you are in your life, you will find a part of yourself in these poems, and you will thank yourself for reading it.** Throughout these pages is the essence of a masterclass in poetry, one that I am excited for Hughes to write."

- Ben Vlam

"No matter the poem, Hughes knows how to use the right words and sentence structure to evoke the most powerful of emotions in the reader. **As you're reading, you feel like Hughes is standing in front of you, telling a story that strikes deep into your heart.** For anyone who wants an emotional read that will keep you fully invested page after page, I highly suggest picking up *Roots of a Girl.*"

- Alessandro Reale, award-winning author

For Dad and Haley, for loving me endlessly

For Khai, for helping me bring myself back to life

For Joyce, and her beautiful soul

But most of all,

For me.

Contents

PREFACE

WHEN I WAS A LITTLE GIRL, I ALWAYS CARRIED around a notebook with me everywhere I went. I was always writing, and I told everyone who would listen that I wanted to write a book one day. Eventually that notebook was lost among my childhood things, and no matter how many times I tried to find it, I couldn't. The years fell away and I became busy with work and life. Eventually a voice creeped in, convincing me that I wasn't good enough to write a book. Who was I among so many others? Poetry is something so visceral, so personal, that it felt terrifying to let anyone else get such an intimate look at my heart.

Eventually that dream took a backseat to other things.

The past two years have taught me so much about growth and self-love and making time for things that feed my soul. I don't think it's a coincidence that then, in that dawn of reconnecting with who it is I am, I found the notebook.

What first began as digitizing my favorite poems soon turned into a newly-remembered love of writing. Then, that snowy January, my heart told me it was finally time to write my book. Now, she's finally ready to breathe.

Roots of a Girl is a poetry collection that explores the shadows of our hearts and the vibrations of our souls. Between all the moments that made us who we are, there was so much life. *Roots of a Girl* shines a light on them all.

This is a journey 30 years in the making. Inside this book are 89 little pieces of my soul.

I hope they find a home with you.

BEGIN

YOU ARE A MOON FLOWER

I hope you learn not to fear
the shadow of the night
but to embrace it
as an old, familiar friend

For growth happens best
not in the chaos of a hurricane,
but in the stillness that
follows after

I hope when storms roll in
and the sun leaves you for a while
you are grateful for the darkness
and lean into it in stride
not in spite of your despair,
but because of it

and you rest in the knowledge
that dawn only comes
after night

My wish for you
is that when night falls heavily
you will not go searching for the sun
but learn instead
to count the stars
for even in your darkest days,
you are the seeds of moon flowers
waiting for permission to bloom

And I -

I am waiting
to lose my breath
at the sight of you.

I Am One with The Night

I am one with the night

So long have I spent in her company
that I no longer fear her talons
or the shaking of her bones
but now ache to hear the honey
that pours from the soft, wide ring
of her throat

She sings for me
and I tell her of you

My Wish for You

I hope one day
you know the peace
of someone who loves you
not in spite of everything that you are not,
but for everything that you are

and I hope

that someone

is you

LOST

LOST

So long have I walked
in the throes of the night
that my own name is lost to
the darkness

I am the empty face
of running water

I am the ghost
of broken dreams

SOLEDAD

I pray you never know the feeling
of sitting in a room,
more alone than anyone else in the universe,
across from the one person
who should have loved you more
than anything
but chose to hate you
instead

THE WALK

At the family outing
my mother came to me
with no question in her voice

Let's take a walk

she said
and I smiled wider than the sun
for the rare treat to feel
like she wanted me there

I glowed upon our return
asking aunts and uncles
"Did you see us leave
together?
Did you wonder where we had been?"

They smiled and said yes
their eyes filled with

what I now know
was heartbreak

I didn't know
that I was just
an excuse to leave
when the tensions rose too high
after the third fight
she had picked that day

I didn't know
that I was not loved,
but used

How positively radiant
I felt to be chosen
as the stress ball
How starved must I have been
to cry with gratefulness
for ten minutes of attention?

Explosions

At ten years old,
I wonder
if any trip to the outside world
won't be marked with
that same violence
that pervades our home

It is hard to care that a parent is sick
when you are too busy
bracing against the bombs

BIRTH DAY

When a child is born,
crying is to be had:
tears of triumph, joy
of new lungs filling with air
and fear of what is to come

But these cries don't belong.
Tears in hushed somberness,
the loneliness,
the wailing.

These are the wrong kind of tears
and they shake me to the bone.

THE CHOICE OF GRIEF

Some say that children
Cannot comprehend death
That they won't understand
The reason they'll no longer
Be greeted at the door

At eight years old
The same was said of me
As I talked to a framed picture of Pop
As if he were still beside me on the couch
How strange, my mother said
That you pretend he's here in the room with you?
She couldn't see the beauty
Of losing someone dear
And letting your love transform
Instead of keeping the ghost of them
In a box too painful to open
And robbing the world of their light

They say that children cannot handle death
But I think that those who doubt
Have forgotten the childlike joy
Of seeing love everywhere
All around you
Asking nothing in return

A Box Containing the Universe

The falsest ships on blackest seas
Show the truth that cannot be
And though these veins were left to bleed,
These eyes that sparkle now can see

A plague of past, two weary eyes,
A tortured smile, a sun to rise
A pain to keep, the urge to run
A loving hand, a life begun

Your words will never leave my head,
Those dancing eyes, that sky of red
But dawn has sent these dreams to bed
Your voice now gone, these hopes all dead

That haunting night, a lasting smile,
A constant dream, a long, long while
My shaking voice, a dance in rain,
A magic touch, a burning stain

A fire I can't bear to tame
A broken chord when I speak your name
A game I never asked to play,
A price I don't have heart to pay

The pain of wails, a bed of stone
A sinking heart, the truth in bone
The weight of sight, a lack of strength
A world away, a gaping length

A screaming louder every day
But farther, farther you slip away
These writhing thoughts take root too deep,
You sowing tears for me to reap

A shadow's spread, a head hung low,
A tired mind, a piercing blow
The curse of truth, a broken lie
A gnawing ache, a love that died

Memories dumped upon the bed
The smell of sand, the taste of dread
The grief of love so long subdued -
It can't hold all
But it does hold you

THE MIMIC

You used to cry about
the hardships you were forced
to suffer
at the hands of those
who should have loved you most

But in all your grief
and anger at their words
you were too busy looking back
to see

that you had done

the very same

to me

I WONDER

i wonder

had i made myself smaller

would i have been enough then?

or only a better size

for trampling on?

A Letter to Adults

Until you understand the vast
loneliness
of a crowded room,
you will never see why children
say nothing
when all they want to do
is scream

I spent years wondering
if this is not normal,
why then does no one speak?
Am I really as invisible
as I feel?
Or is it simply
that no one cares?

I never learned the answer
or asked what they would say
but now that I am older,
this is all I know:

I won't fail them
like you failed
me

HAUNTED

ABANDONMENT

You realized I wasn't a doll
dipped in compliance and silver dust
waiting to be bent your whim
so you turned your back on me forever,
the most unnatural loneliness there is

I have spent the rest of my life
banging my fists on your memory:

"I exist, I exist, I exist"

CONFESSIONAL

It is easy as breathing
for most
to love their mother
But for me it felt like
being on fire
all the time
and hiding from the gasoline
she poured on my entire life

How can someone who disappeared
still make you shake when darkness comes?

I will spend my days
taking deeper breaths
and fighting off the damage caused
until the end of time
And that is a war crime
for which she can never be forgiven

This is my confession
for which I must atone:
the sound of her feet
walking out of my life
was the sweetest sound
I've ever known.

TRAUMA

My body aches
from the earthquakes through my bones
and tornadoes ripping through
my nerves,
tearing down the house of twigs
I am constantly rebuilding
and I wonder
how many nights of my life
will be spent shaking too hard to sleep?
Surely I have borne the load
enough
for lifetimes

SOMEWHERE IN SLEEP

Somewhere in sleep,
you find me
in a dark and terrible dream

How long must I beg
until you leave me in peace?

ASHES

When you stoked the fires and fanned them
into rage
I thought it my job to keep all kindling
out of sight and far from your reach
What else will a child do?
Not knowing that in your pocket
lay the matches
you made a choice to strike

I might spend the rest of my life
finding forgiveness for you
for burning down the walls
of the only home
you let me have

FEAR OF SILENCE

Some fear silence for the loneliness,
others for its boredom

But when you live in a war zone
silence is a rare
and precious
gift

WHAT A CHILD SHOULD NOT HAVE TO DO

I never learned to protect my peace
because I was called in to bear witness,
to be judge and jury,
to be peacekeeper and distraction
since the day I was born.

No wonder I cannot help
but make others' problems
my own

THE CURSE

I am so tired
from the weight
on my shoulders
that all girls carry into womanhood,
that all women reel against

I am tired from
fighting for existence
and screaming to be heard
while men simply get to breathe.

PROTECTOR

Through all the tears
and weight of sobs,
the heavy blows of second guessing
if I had done enough,
if I had done too much,
if it was not my place -

At least I will breathe
knowing someone
had done
something

APATHY

I spent so long enforcing locks
and shutting windows tight
not against the chill,
but against the slinking fox
prowling outside in the night
that I turned red with grief to realize
that it was the hen herself
who let him back in

TAKER

You lured me in
with promise of a place
to rest my head,
drank freely from
the pools
of honeysuckle warmth
until your bones
were healed anew

But I left feeling like drowned cotton
wrung by angry hands
used and then tossed aside
to decompose
in shame of the dirt beneath my skin

How long will it take you to learn
that that is war
not love?

STAR-CROSSED

I used to think that when you fell in love,
There was nothing left to find but babies
And candles on the cake
So imagine how,
When I met you,
I started counting

I didn't know then
That when I saw you through the roses
I was really watching you on a distant shore
Standing on the wrong side of an ocean
That cannot be crossed

In a universe freckled with worlds,
Maybe there is one where you and I don't wither
Like old flowers, forgotten in the heat
But in this one,

We are a flame fighting to stay alive
Against a winter storm,
Orpheus and Eurydice,
Ill-fated from the start

We were the distance between stars,
The darkened power of a hurricane

Terrifying

And beautiful

All at once

SOMEWHERE BETWEEN DREAMS

Somewhere
between dreams
are the scattered hopes
and promises,
tossed aside to wilt,
with the plans that we made
and the words that you said
decaying in the graveyard
of young love
and bitter ends

And somewhere
between dreams,
your smile haunts me always

For while the pieces of my heart
lay as ashes in the dirt,
every one of them
calls out for you
still

Rare & Precious Thing

Perhaps it's for the best
that your heart doesn't breathe for me
the way I do for you -

I wouldn't know what to do
holding a star in my hands

TIRED

So many times have I stirred, thinking

This feels like the beginning

only to watch
my tears fall
in the end

THE ARBOR

It's not intentional
how I still sleep
at the edge
of the bed
leaving space for
where you used to lie

When you live day by day
in shared presence
with another
you grow around the hole
they leave when they
are gone
the patterns of their breath
falling still
across your back

I wonder if I will always
go on like this
Hardened vines
too rigid now against
the shape of you
as if my limbs
know for what they ache,
as if even my body
remembers
you should be here

SPECTRE

A ghost haunts these walls
Following me from room to room
A reminder of what was once before
But can never be again

I feel his presence
Like frost upon the window
A whisper of an echo
From years and years ago
So soft and barely there
But the cold of snow-flecked glass
Still chills me to the bone

I am haunted by distant music
And the ache of long-gone smiles
Wondering how we went from dancing in the kitchen
To grieving in its emptiness

At every turn, footsteps follow me
No matter how far or how long I run
Like a shadow I can't be rid of
A despair I never asked for
Like a cancer of the heart
Every moment in solitude a dose
Of poison coursing through my veins

I could fill the seas
With tears that I have cried
For the ghost of a man
Who sits just down the hall
For while he still draws breath
He has long since gone to death
His chosen home a graveyard
Of the love he drowned in the depths

MISMATCHED

How strange a thing
that you live every day
knowing each beat of my heart
speaks your name
and I don't even
know where you are?

PINING

I don't dream
he'll change his mind;

I dream the day
I read the words

I now know
the same pain
I caused you

And you
were
right

DECEIVER

You lured me into love
and promised to hold my heart in yours,
but just as our roots entangled,
you turned to ashes
and slipped through my fingers
before I even smelled the smoke

You tell me not to worry
that I'll find someone who loves me
as if your wreckage doesn't devastate
the very breath that enters my lungs

But tell me, *All Knowing One,*
what tree can stay standing with its moorings
ripped away with such violence?

What hope can come from such ruin?

Only Love Keeps Me Here

I grow so weary
from holding off the waves
fighting to resurface
just to tumble down again
It is exhausting
crawling from the depths of darkness
and I am so, so tired
of holding up my head

But my strength cannot fail me now
for if I gave in to
the lulling of the night,
those who love me
would be doomed to it forever

And that is a curse
I will not pass on

HEALING

STIRRING

There's a rumbling in me
like thunder
rolling and twisting
through the valley
shaking trees
until they are left bewildered
and bare

Something stirs
like fat water droplets
falling in mud
on summer nights
creating explosions

I ache for ocean air
and to feel the legs
that have conquered a mountain

To fall to my knees beneath
the stars
and kiss the wind
like an old
familiar lover

My hands plead for dirt and work
and my feet lust to take me
farther
than I have ever gone
before

I am not sustained
by water
if it does not come
from a river
that carries me in its arms

My lungs grow weak
from holding nothing
but air
when they cry out
to feel the release
of a roar

The sound of sameness
louder than
the fiery sea
crashes through my ears

like a million crickets in a jar
fearful
and begging to be free

I am starving for the sunrise
for so many days of my life
I have missed it
as I slept
in my bed

I am tired
of exhaustion
and my bones are breaking
under the weight
of empty days
and bitter news

I do not know anything
but that
the land
of milk and honey
tastes sour in my mouth
and I must go

Somewhere

and anywhere

but here.

HEALING

I feel the grief and loneliness
of being the only one
who loves me;

I am still learning
that this is more
than enough

PLEASE FIND ME

Will you know me
when the rains come
and the salt of the earth
is washed from my skin,
when my feet lift from the ground
and I toss wildly,
lost in the winds of the storm
in the night?

Will you know me?

WINTER STARS

You know the smell of a winter night?
You walk outside
and feel the crisp, cold air on your skin
that takes your breath away
and at first, you wonder why you're even there
when the shelter of inside is so close at hand

But the night is so clear and so, so silent
Your body melts into a stillness you've never known
and you can physically taste the cold in the air
Suddenly, the peace that you've been yearning for
all your life
is there, everywhere, all at once

And oh my god, the stars

You've never seen stars like this before.
A thousand freckles in the sky,

so lonely and far
but forever part of something
great
and meaningful
and true
Joined by a million miles of serenity
and adopted kin

As you walk,
you're bathed in pure, white light from the moon
like the milk of skin that glows with love
and you feel warm arms around you
A hug from the whole universe
And you feel, for the first time in so long,
that you are loved

So don't you see?
No matter how badly
you want to go,
you have to make it past the fall;

You can only taste the stars in the wintertime.

And that, dear love,
is a beauty
worth staying for.

ACHILLES' HEALING

I am learning
how to hide the keys
that open the doors
to my soft underbelly

Too many times
have I been hung
by knots
tied in good faith
by my own hands

RELEASE

I release you of the burden
you carry like cinder blocks
with broken knees:

All you could do was survive
and that was enough

THE SHADOW OF THE DARKNESS

You used to follow me in every step
the shadow at my side
whenever hope drew near

How can I trust
that he won't be the same
when last time
I didn't see the danger
until I was too far within its depths?

When butterflies began to grow
the sight of your face
made my legs want to run
and it took strength immeasurable
to stand still long enough
to give the roots a chance to grow

I have made a choice
to not let you haunt me anymore;
Too long have you perched on my shoulder
pushing me to fear.

I choose instead
to fly

WOUNDS OF RELIEF

Each night, I sharpen knives
before I sleep
open festering wounds down to the bone
to scrape away the traces you left
raked across my skin

Unlocking horrors from the depths of my mind
is more agony than you'll ever know
but I'd rather feel the fire
of debrided flesh
scrubbed clean of your face
than love for someone
who doesn't want me in return

TIME TRAVELER

I think about all the things I would have said
if this new healing version of me
could go back and speak through
the little girl crying herself to sleep,
the twenty-year-old who still thought
being polite was more important
than being safe

I am so angry
that I couldn't be there
to fight for them

GUILT

I long ago
released the guilt
that came with talking
to my heart
and willing it to finally speak:

With you here, I was suffocating
And with you gone, I am free

And I am glad

that you are dead

FOR HALEY

Once toddlers
in the schoolyard
now wrinkled women
holding hands through life
This is the most
beautiful
and cherished story
of my days

In any lifetime,
I would have found you
and I will
in all of those to come
Our sisterhood knows not
blood or boundaries,
only the ease of sun-warmed water
and the strength of deepened roots

We were born of stardust
and of honeysuckle
from the light of the same moon -
timeless
and endless
as the sea

A Mother's Misconception

You saw my love as weakness
a menacing threat to be stamped out

You couldn't understand kindness
not for gain, but for beauty
You held up a shattered mirror
and painted it in black
until I, too, ran
from the learned shame of a soft heart

We always fear what we have never known

But my kindness
took the flowers you trampled
and sang to them until they grew

whispered to them
until they stood tall again
just like it did
for me

REVENGE

I have done more
than just survive you.

I am bursting at the seams
with love

When You Cannot Turn Away

One day
when the house isn't burning
and the ground doesn't shake
beneath your feet,
you will understand
why I stood my ground
and screamed,
why I held you in the grass,
sobbing together under the clouded sky,
and I begged you not to go.

When you see those same violet marks
on the snow-white cheek
of someone you love,
you will know
why I held you tight against the floor,

immune to the scratches and shrieks,
the desperation of a victim
ripped from the safety of thorns,
and refused to let you run back
into the danger of the lion's den.

Your tears will fall like mine
as they beg to be set free
and you are forced to do

anything,

anything,

everything

to keep them away from those black eyes,
that furious body poised to pounce
to do anything you can
to keep them alive.

Yes, your tears will fall like mine
as you feel the weight of love
and you will come to understand:
I had no other choice.

UNIVERSAL

It occurred to me then
that there must not be a woman alive
who is happy with her appearance
and in that moment
I decided to be content
instead of racing towards a finish line
that is impossible to cross

THE LESSON ALL GIRLS LEARN

The need to save things
Had always bound my heart
As much as it had filled it with joy
While I smiled at the drowning bee
Rescued from the death grip of the pond,
I wept for the tiny bird pushed from the nest
Not to fly, but to be gone
Diseased, perhaps, or one too many;
I doubt it mattered much to him

I grieved for the fawn I found in the yard,
Much too late for helping
And was haunted by the sound of a cat
Too far to find, but close enough
That I could hear its cries
As it left its suffering earth side

It wasn't just animals, but people
I tried to save
And it took years of nightmares
To learn that not all humans are worth saving

I was too young to understand,
Too scarred by others' hardships
That I found myself more than once
Trapped within a spider's web
Unaware that it was I who needed rescuing
Like the bees tangled in the duckweed
My sights so set on the job at hand
That I failed to see the water rise around me

It was then that I learned this truth
That humans are rare and strange
In that they cannot be saved by others,
But only by themselves

For it was I who ignored the calls
Of those trying to break me free
And after years of torment finally saw
That it was I who needed
To put one foot in front of the other
Through the fields of heavy mud
To climb from darkness

The need to save things
Still breaks my heart
But I have learned to tell the difference
Between the rabbit in the predator's jaws
And the fox waiting
With his mouth open wide

SURVIVOR

She is not a flower
that you can bully into silence
Afraid to lose her petals
as you threaten to shake them loose

She is a thunderstorm
Wild
and brimming with fury
more powerful than your worst
nightmares

And you have set

    Her winds

      Ahowling

VOICES OF MY SISTERS

I shook with fury
as I loosed arrows drenched in poison
at the darkness in the doorway,
fearing nothing but the headlines
my complicity could render

I stood taller than an oak tree,
trembling but rooted
by the heartache of my sisters
as we pull our arms together
and shield our backs in turn

Their voices lifted through me
as I rumbled through the hallway
Words that echo through the centuries
of womanhood and fear,

words that stand upon the bones
of every woman forced to silence
with no one to
speak up for her

THE GARDEN IS MY FRIEND

It's a strange feeling,
Being a child surrounded
By friends and grown ups
Numerous as birds in the sky
And still feeling utterly

Alone

While they tried to weave a tapestry
To carry me to the sky,
The embodiment
Of fortitude
That should have been mine by right,
You ran around with scissors,
Pulling at every thread

So I turned to walk the garden
And found that here,

My singing was never silenced
But echoed instead in tune
And the cool rush of pond water
Made me glad to be alive
And if the lilies could grow through the soil,
Then by god, so could I
And the wind hugged me close
The way you never did

I learned long ago that
the only place to find peace
Within your walls
Was inside myself
As I created it

THE BURDEN OF BEAUTY

"Beauty is pain,"
my mother used to yell
as she dug under my fingernails
or forced me into tights

I'd hear it as my tears ran from the mascara
she was sure were needed
on five-year-old eyelashes,
my cheeks covered in blush
as my brother ran freely outside
for what is a tutu
without a beautiful doll within it?

I'd hear it so often that it seemed a truth to her
that a woman must be beautiful

in order to be
whole
or valued
or loved
and therefore, a girl must suffer

A mother's duty, I'm sure she felt
but she never stopped to ask
if beauty was something I wanted
or if I cared about the way strangers
felt about my face

If it would have bothered me that I wasn't thin
(thin *enough*, in her eyes)
if she didn't remind me every day
or if I wanted to be known
by the way my lips looked iparn a polite smile
as I made myself small enough to dodge the arrows
she was sure were waiting

She never asked, but if she had
I'd tell her I wanted to be known
for the way I sang in the garden
or held my friends close in sorrow,
the fire in my eyes on the field
as I learned I could run and do it well.
What is beauty if you cannot show mercy to an insect?
or throw your head back in blissful laughter,

stay up to see the sunrise
and be brave enough to go searching
and finally know who it is you are?

"Beauty is pain,"
my mother used to yell.
And now that she is gone,
I'd give anything to pull her close and whisper

Beauty is nothing
compared to you.

A LETTER TO ALL GIRLS

Trust that fire
in your belly -

It is the voices of
past sisters
and they will not
steer you wrong

PARDONED

Some days
I have strength enough
to conquer mountains

and on others
just enough
to lift my head

Both days
I have done enough

THE ALCHEMIST

She dipped the quill
into the ink of her soul
and let the words
pull the poison from her veins -

The way the page
embraced her tears
was the only love
she'd ever known

THE THINGS I DO KNOW

I do not know all the answers
to all the questions
plaguing my heart,
do not do the right things
or say the perfect words
in every moment.

But I do know how
to take the shaking
of a loved one's sobs
and calm them into
quiet breaths,
to walk among the daffodils
overwhelmed by beauty
and moved to tears
with gratitude.
My legs will never fail
as I stand tall to face

a raging beast
and my words carry sweetness
from the honeysuckle bush
growing wild in the woods
I used to roam

In times of darkness
when love for myself
is as small as a raindrop,
my heart whispers softly

Isn't that enough?

A Haunting I'm Glad Of

I used to ask for help, aching to know
How do you sleep knowing there is so much
suffering in the world?
The faces of gaunt children and crying babies
haunt me in the night,
sounds I wish I could forget
but never will

How can I sleep here, soft in my bed
knowing the fingers of despair
are weaving their way through innocent lives
this very moment?

What have I done,
I used to ask,
to deserve this life?

I do not know the answer, but what I learned in time
is that love doesn't come from guilt,
but from power
and maybe I wasn't lucky in this life,
but chosen

Chosen not to avoid the horror,
but to break it
My legs, strong from years of life,
can carry others when their legs fail,
my shoulders, proud and tall,
can be a place to rest their heads
until they too can stand again
my voice, so easily heard
in my skin of milk and joy,
can scream and raise the mountains
until not one person can claim
they have not seen
the shadows

I used to ache to know through tears,
dying to know how anyone sleeps
with the weight of everything
on their backs
But now I rest not despite my guilt,
but from the ease
of knowing my hands have gone to work

I cannot do it all, I say
but I have done what I can
for tonight.

FAITH

My heart knows
that I question her
every time I stitch her
back together
and she pleads to try again
once the tears have finally
dried

It'll be worth it,

she says

I know,

I say

THE LONELINESS

On the nights my tears
well onto the pillow
and I tell myself
there's no more use in trying,

I wonder if a man out there
feels the same
not knowing we are destined
for each other

I wonder if we stare up
at the same moon
and let our tears fill
the ocean between us,
not convinced the other exists,
but deciding we owe them
at least the chance to try

Two Sides of a Broken Coin

Between storms that shook the house
and forcing my lungs to search
for deeper breaths
your laughter tinkled through the hallways
like a bell,
the same laugh I now loose freely.
When not noticing my every flaw
we looked for fairies in the garden
peaking over primroses
creating the joy you never knew

Your fire at injustice
helped grow the roaring voice
I hold
Much the same way it grew
after you stifled it for years

It was you who helped me see
the beauty of the wind
the reason tears well at the painted dawn
The same way they fall
at the loneliness
you engraved within my bones

You are both the best of me
and the shadow that haunts me
in the night

How strange, I think,
that you can be both things at once?

THE WISH

And I asked her

What if the best thing
that happens to you
this year
is that you fall in love
with yourself?

She said
that was all
she'd ever
wanted

DAYLILIES

The daylilies grow wild
on the hillside where I was raised
nestled between raspberry brambles
and mossy fallen trees
peeking out of their year-long beds
ready to stretch towards the sun
There is no one to tend them
but the earth and sky and stars
and yet they grow free and without a shred of doubt
They cozy together among their sisters
and for them, that is nourishment enough

I want to be a daylily
and thrive in any soil
needing no man to tend me
but the sun upon my face
my wildness my strength
and my sisters' arms my home

questioning not whether I am wanted
or if I have permission to exist
but how deep I can grow my roots
and whether this place is worthy
of the beauty I bestow

The daylilies shower the hillsides
in beauty and self-truth
and the song of belonging they carry
will lift me to better days
ahead

SILVER LINING

I have long since gone to bed
and closed my eyes for rest
but slumber finds me not
as I toss within the sheets
And so instead,
I dream

I dream of moonlit nights when the sky was ever clear
his arms around my chest, holding me tight
I breathe in warmth and comfort
as he shows me the river where
he used to play

I dream of sun-kissed hours
and the smell of old books
as we wander through the stacks,
touching spines, touching hands,
our eyes only on each other

I meander through the feeling
of hands holding my face,
gentle as a dove
the touch of ease and love
as hazel eyes stare into mine
our foreheads pressed together

I dream of tears shed like a waterfall
as he held me tight against my sobs
his tears falling in my hair
as we knew we had to say goodbye

You made me love myself
he said

You gave me safety
I said

and we agreed

We weren't meant to last forever,
but meant to leave each other
these precious gifts
instead

CHRYSALIS

Your grief is not a stone meant to drown you
and crush you under its weight;

It is a chrysalis.

It is a changing wind biding its time
until the rain doesn't feel like lonely knives
but soft kisses on your face

Until sleepless nights and frozen tears
turn to wonder at the stars
and the darkness feels not like suffocation,
but being held by warmth and velvet

One day, you'll see a sunrise
and feel not just the pang of loss
but the wind in your hair
and the soft tips of summer grass in your hands
As the pink light fills your heart

you'll realize they *are* the sun
that shines upon your face each day

You'll find them in the belly laughs
and late nights that feel like magic
and soon, your homeless love will overflow
and soak the ground in joy and kindness

Your grief will grow wings
and you'll give them away
and there is nothing
more beautiful
than that

My dear child,
Don't you see?

Love never dies;
it only transforms.

CROCUSES

It is a strange thing
to see the purple crocus petals
peeking out among the snow,
beauty existing
where it should not be able to survive

I saw them as a sign, that day
as I stepped off into the unknown,
trusting that the fall
would be worth it
that I, too, would not be left
to wither in the wind
without the embrace of the universe
helping me to bloom
where I thought
impossible

As the year turns around again
and the petals make their way to the sun
I realize that the crocuses
were right

For where else can strength grow
if not from the mud of bitter winters?

HOPE

SEEDS

At some point we finally understand
that when we were buried
we were really planted,
when the rain came
we quietly started to grow.

What a beautiful gift that comes
from the tempest of the storm

AESTHETE

If given the chance
to live
a life with fewer
sorrows
I'd still choose to be
a dreamer
moved to tears
by the beauty
of the rain

No peace of mind
is worth giving up
the joy
of a life felt
this deeply

TELL HIM

The truth you hide
weighs not as shackles on your hands

Your truth is a gift

It is yours to share,
to hold close,
to bestow

No matter the fear
that makes you quake,

Let it free
Let it fall
Let it *fly*

THE FIRST

The night sighed into rhythm,
the storm brewing for ages
finally calmed into peace

One star twinkled in the distance

The night holding its breath
for the words many months in the making
finally released to be free

A rush of hope and prayers
entwined together in the courage of darkness
came tumbling out like a waterfall
that had been dammed up for years

The warmth of the words came pouring out
like honey in a summer wind
to wrap them up in velvet arms

I love you
he said

And I love you

And the one star twinkled on.

LAURIE

I met a woman on the street
Who told me to see the beauty in all things

The world is a love letter from God,
She said
Nothing matters in the world
Except a wild love of him
And showing his love through our hands
In all we do and touch.

Do not fear the unknown,
she said;
He is as near to us as our breath.

I have never believed in a power
That could hold the universe together

But if I believed in any god,
In any force so strong,
It would be the heart of kindness
That adorns people like her.

Deeply, Truly

As a girl,
I was taught to have
a wish list miles long
for the man who
earned my heart

But the truth is
you could stand there
doing nothing at all
and I'd still swear the sun
shines brighter
because you draw
breath

WAITING

I dreamed you once
When I climbed high into the magnolia tree
And whispered, *"God, give me someone to love."*

I dreamed you in the winter sky
Under ink-black frost and starlight
Through guiding light of ivory moons,
I felt you near.

I loved you before the oceans sang
And the mountains crashed to life
A thousand times, I fell in love
Before You and I and They
We'd not yet begun to be,
But I loved you still

I carried you with me through wild lands
Feeling the earth breathe beneath my feet

And my own breath, for the first time
As I loved you

I dreamed you in the autumn rains
And fire's light
In the flicker, arms wrapped close,
You whispered
"Soon, Love, soon"

Each year the magnolia lifted her arms
And whispered beauty into the world
I waited, knowing she'd carry you to me
In the wind
And sweet scent of lilacs

I waited

And there you were,
And I knew.

For I had dreamed you all my life.

GARDEN TENDER

Don't forget,
Dear love,
That you are the tenderness that
Grows the flowers in the garden
For while they naturally grow beautiful,
They cannot take root
Without your care

You are both the
Storm of strength
That makes seas rise
And teaches young girls to stand tall
And the gentle wind
That seasoned women delight in
As you run through their hair
reminding them they are enough

Your warmth is the joyful feeling
Of bare skin drying in the sun
And those in grief
Thank god for you
As the clouds part and they turn their faces
Towards your light
To feel alive again

Dear love,
Don't forget:
There is no beauty in the world
Without you

ETERNITY IN A MOMENT

You held me
long before the threat of dawn
brushed your lips on mine
your hands tangled in my hair
I didn't care what else
the day may bring
because in that moment
I knew that this was life

enough

for

years

You Are a Lighthouse

Soft kisses fall like drops of rain
from wind in the leaves
as storms give way and sunlight sets in
A gentle and joyful reminder
of you here

A breath of winter sky,
cold and beautiful in my lungs
as I sit outside
and the moon and stars
wrap me in peace like your arms
with a clearness I have never known

A belly laugh
like the racing
of feet on pavement
and endless days of summertime

The thrill and joy
of now
so light and glowing
in my heart

Your fingers on my skin
caressing with warm eyes
like dew drops in the morning
and the rising sun on my face
as I walk aimlessly, anywhere
feeling the earth and soft whispers
on my fingertips
from grasses tall as I
as for once,
the world is quiet

When seas rise
and I'm lost in
waves of darkness
you are the lighthouse
and the current
that pulls me into shore
and holds me, deep and true,
until the skies clear,
my tears are dried
and I can face the day
anew

THE PROMISE OF THE DAWN

Tears well into flowering thyme
Grateful from the fated start
That honeyed eyes, so soft and kind
Should rest upon my heart

Your scent entangled in my hair
As a moth upon paned glass
The feel of moonlight in the air,
The dew upon the grass

A head at rest upon my own
Fends darkness and the night
A tenderness I've never known
That brings me to the light

You are the promise of the dawn,
The snowmelt in the spring
The peace of everlasting song
That only love can bring

LYING IN WAIT

I think
"There is beauty in the withered things"
as I fill a jar with vines
That long since passed from life to dust
Their leaves in tattered lines

The faded petals of the rose
Still blush through sullied hues
Much richer now, as summer fades;
A deeper shade anew

The lark hates not the barren branch
As a seat to loose its song
The fallow field and crumbling stone
To the earth still do belong

If deadened beds can teem with life,
Still hold a cherished view,
There is hope for times we slumber by;
The garden speaks it true.

CHANGED

I rest for a time
In the laurels of your graces
and emerge anew in the dawn of your smile
A mere glimpse of you
can lift any darkness

There are few things
I wouldn't give
to hold you close,
listen to the thrumming of your heart
in the soft pool of night
or trade the comforts of my life
to shield you from the pain of yours

I cannot breathe without your name on my lips,
cannot dream without your face
I am consumed by you
in the most irrevocable way -

Always you will be carried by my soul

WANDERING

Of all
of my
adventures
coming home
to you
was the
greatest

I KNOW YOUR FACE

From my wall of windows, I watch the rain fall
into the grass and listen to the sound of the leaves
sighing with the weight of it.
It brings me such comfort to know that trees, too,
bear weight upon their shoulders.
They didn't ask for it, either, and even knowing
that it will water their roots -
as it will with mine -
I wonder if they, too, tremble in the wind,
wondering if they have strength enough
to stand through it.

How curious a thing it is, what we humans do,
thinking ourselves
such rare creatures that we are the only ones
who fear loneliness
or let our tears fall like raindrops in the dirt.
Do you not think that vines ache to climb higher

or that deer peer around after stumbling to know
if anyone has seen?
The magnolia tree weeps for the dropped petals of her
long-labored blooms
and somewhere in the forest, a raspberry bush is so
very, very tired
from turning its fruits inwards
from the ravenous birds
in the same way that I am, too.

We are all of us the same, here in this universe,
all made of the dust and dreams of stars.
Our heartbreak and our weariness transcend
any separation we are foolish enough
to believe exists
between the troubles of the earthworm and ourselves

Is it not a beautiful thing to be so known
by everything around us?

Darling Love

There is something precious about love,
I muse, some sweet purity
bathed in moonlit white
as my world flutters at the sound
of his voice full of kindness,
gentle like he were cooing to a dove
held steady within his hands

There exists in all the world
nothing more dear
than the feeling of my bursting heart
drumming against my chest
at the sight of the way he looks at me
my joy radiant
as the stars shine out from my eyes

Repose

I have never felt so free
as feeling blades of grass
beneath my toes
The cool earth
rising up to reassure me
that I am welcome in her home

We made a world of rules
and struggling to survive,
a sea of expectations waiting
to swallow us whole
It is easy to forget
that we intrinsically belong,
we are a part of nature
and can always come back
home

GIFTS AT THE DOOR

Along the winding path,
footprints to the door
and the familiar scent
of marigolds
tell me someone I know
was here
Gifts adorn the doorway
from each memory of me

A teddy, from myself
at six years old
sits beside a gilded note:
You can't see it now,
but these days
are few
and ending
and soon your pain
will turn to love;

She left me the one I'd hug
through the loneliness

Beside it lays a ticket
to the coffee house
a gift to remember the night
that I sang,
the last days of sixteen
with my father in the audience
fielding questions on the whereabouts
of the mother I hadn't seen in months
She chose to forget she had children
so I chose not to ask her to come

The flowers from my senior prom
waiting patiently
in a crystal vase
for me to recall the ache
when I, just barely eighteen
was so tired of being alone
that I'd give my love to anyone
and realized too late
that a man of darkness
had swallowed me whole.
She wrote that I more deserved
the flowers now
for climbing from within his gullet

The gifts continued on
A loving trail of joy and pride

To say *forget not,*
you are the one who has climbed mountains
the breath of the earth lives in your eyes

LOVE OF MY LIFE

Somewhere along the way
the understanding finally grew:

I am my greatest love of all

Waiting For the Day

I finally gave up wondering one day
what my wedding would be like,
what kind of lace I'd run my fingers through
and the flowers that would adorn my hair
lovingly looking into the eyes
of a faceless groom

Sometimes he took shape
and I felt it in my bones
but each time that vision turned to dust
and he became a blur once again

The hope of that is gone for now
and I began to dream instead
of the calm breaths of the ocean
as I stand there and feel the changing wind
I dream now of
the warm embrace of solitude

knowing now that it is not desolation
but peace and power
I dream of the laughter of friends
and the smiles of strangers
the joy that I can bring
and the joy that I can find

Perhaps one day
that dream will once again take root
but I've stopped waiting for the day,
missing life all the while;

I do not need a reason
to wear flowers in my hair

THE LEAF THAT FELL PERFECTLY

I don't know if you can hear me,
if you're there
If that was you who placed a falling leaf
perfectly upon the page I write on
right as I thought that I can feel you
in this moment
as the setting sun turns golden
and the warm air is filled with the gentle sound
of wind rushing through the autumn leaves

I hold the leaf in my fingers
and close my eyes as I start to cry
What a hug from the universe,
a sign that you're here

A gift to thank me for thinking of you

I don't know if you can hear me
but I feel you listening now
as if you stood right there in the ivy

This is one of those moments
where your presence
rings clear as a bell

I pause a moment to feel you
I open my mouth to speak

Nothing but a whisper leaves
but I know for you, it is loud enough
when I almost never speak your name

I am trying to let my grace and kindness
seep into every crevice of your memory
to take my pain and grief
and breathe out compassion
instead

I am not perfect
and I'm sorry for the days anger wins

I am trying.

Thank you for
the moments you
loved me
Today, that is enough

THE ROSEBUSH

When my mother died,
I drowned
The grief and chaos like a storm
The violent winds so strong
my feet were lifted from my stronghold
tossed around like a stone
and forced to stare it in the face

She departed in her sleep
and left me tumbling in the waves
of anger and despair

I didn't know what to do
except to spread my love like wildflowers
in every corner of her being
in every place touched by the sun
with her long, winding fingers

To give my love away
was the only way through
the darkness

I spoke gently and lived truly
found myself in the light of others' faces
and let their glow of joy
illuminate the poison
from within
I gave her away in pieces
What else could I have done?

We chose a poem for her grave
that talked of living on in flowers
Of eternity in the growth of roots
from the marrow of her memory
I couldn't bear the naked ground
of dry earth, cracked and turned
when she should have flowers in her hair
and the light upon her face
the wind in the palms of her hands
and the soft touch of morning dew

One day I needed solace
and planted the smallest rosebush I ever saw
at her feet
Let my hands turn the earth

to bury something in warmth
instead of night

I never asked permission
I didn't know if it would grow
I tucked her in with a tiny prayer
and let my tears sink
to water her toes

As the sun turned
around and around
and the days fell into months,
into years,
I seldom found strength enough
to walk up to her grave
But others did.

And oh, how they loved her.

As the rosebush grew
so, too, did her visitors
to witness their grief transformed,
to care for my mother once again
in the soft smiles of remembrance
caress the perfect tendrils of her leaves

and whisper all the words
left unsaid

She drew caretakers far and wide -
many I never even knew -
driving hours to prune her leaves
and see her petals
to visit her on dark days
and find a place to rest their
wandering love
so glad of shelter and new walls
after so many days stumbling blindly
in the night

We, too, were nourished by
her growth
as she climbed on and on
to the stars

What a beautiful thing she has become
a shining diamond in the dark
waiting to listen and to hold us
as we are joined by memories in stride

I went to my mother's grave today

For the first time in
I don't know how many
months or years

I gasped at the sight of her
standing tall in the golden sun
adorned by blushing baubles
at the face of the warm brown stone

How profound, I think
that even in the first burn ban
I have ever seen
when all else is dry and dead as dust
and the trees stand naked in the wind
the rosebush is filled with perfect blooms
that reach up to the sky?

She is untouched by normal days,
I recall;

Her roots were grown
by love.

ACKNOWLEDGEMENTS

There truly is nothing that would exist without the unseen support of other people. I may be the author, but this book would not have been possible without the work of so many quiet hands behind the scenes. Please allow me to shine a lot on all of these wonderful people who have helped make *Roots of a Girl* and asked for nothing in return.

Thank you to Lara Fowler at The Quote House for taking an incomplete kernel of an idea and creating the most beautiful and meaningful book cover I have ever seen. She truly read my mind at every step, went above and beyond with adjustments, and created something better than I could have ever hoped for.

Thank you to Blumen House for the gorgeous illustrations that grace some of the pages of *Roots of a Girl*. They truly add that extra special touch to the reading experience and blend in perfectly with the collection.

Most of all, thank you to the countless people who have supported me or cheered me on in some small way. It would be impossible to name everyone who has shown love for me and for this book, and I am beyond grateful for it all. Some of those who have been the most invested and provided the most encouragement and time during this process are Haley, Joelle, Audrey, Ben, Sophie, Alessandro, Ian, and Kate. Thank you, thank you, thank you for all the love and support you have shown me.

And finally, I want to say thank you to you.

A book written is always an accomplishment, but a book read is something altogether more special. Thank you for finding something in this book worth reading and helping to put breath in her lungs. I hope she stays with you.

ABOUT THE AUTHOR

Meghan Hughes is a Philadelphia-based author and *Roots of a Girl* is her debut published work. She has worked in education for many years and loves inspiring others, especially children, to make the world a better place and protect our natural world. She is also an award-winning professional photographer and has earned many accolades for her artistic vision. You can often find her wandering the famous gardens of Philadelphia, where she finds much of her inspiration for her writing. She lives with her friends, her cat, Iris, and her many dreams.

www.MeghanHughesWriting.com

www.ingramcontent.com/pod-product-compliance
Lightning Source LLC
Chambersburg PA
CBHW071248130626
46556CB00003B/1212